W9-AHG-959

The Reader

a screenplay by

David Hare

WEINSTEIN
BOOKS

Copyright © 2009 David Hare

All rights reserved. No part of this book may be used or reproduced in
any manner whatsoever without the written permission of the Publisher.
Printed in the United States of America. For information address
Weinstein Books, 345 Hudson Street, 13th Floor, New York, NY 10014.

ISBN 978-1-60286-093-3

First Edition
10 9 8 7 6 5 4 3 2 1

The Reader

Introduction

Long before film-makers of any nationality began their attempts to offer fictionalised drama about the Holocaust, then the French director Jean-Luc Godard made a famous statement: "If ever a film is to be made about Auschwitz, it will have to be from the point of view of the guards."

I would love to be able to claim that Godard's remark came immediately to mind when I first read Bernard Schlink's novel *The Reader* on its original publication in the English language in 1998. If it had, it would most certainly have been appropriate. Like so many people in the United Kingdom, I had first heard of the book when I read George Steiner's recommendation in *The Observer;* "A masterly work . . . The reviewer's sole and privileged function is to as say as loudly as he is able, 'Read this' and 'Read it again.'" Since nobody had ever imagined Steiner was a critic who would praise any modern novel lightly, this ringing endorsement was especially striking. I went out and bought the book at once.

The reason *The Reader* made such a strong impression and became such a success throughout the world was because it did genuinely open a new field of inquiry. It had already taken a long time for the suffering of Jews in the European concentration camps of the 1930s and 1940s to reach deep into public consciousness. In the twenty years immediately after the end of the war, there was an understandable reluctance among survivors to describe in any detail what they had been through. It was as if a seemly reticence were the only available response to murder on such a previously unimagined scale. In Israel, in particular, the resolve to build a new country meant that older people were not encouraged to talk about the past. Often, indeed, people felt ashamed of having come through when so many of their families and fellow inmates had been killed. When Primo Levi's *If This is a Man* was first published soon after the war, then most of the 2,500 copies printed mouldered unsold in an Italian warehouse.

If in Israel it was the appearance and conviction of Adolf Eichmann in Jerusalem in 1961 which brought about a decisive shift in public understanding, then it was the Auschwitz trials in Frankfurt between 1963 and 1965—realised through the persistence of one lone prosecutor Fritz Bauer—which had a comparable impact in Germany. Thirty years after those trials, it was Bernard Schlink's singular achievement as a lawyer conceiving his first non-detective novel to invent a narrative which finally articulated the dilemma of so many Germans who were born, through no fault of their own, as the children of a great crime. How does a succeeding generation deal with the transgressions of their parents? How do they find a way of living anything like a normal life? *The Reader* is not simply a novel specific to the post-war German experience. It is also a more far-reaching exploration of the painful and difficult process we all now know under the name of truth and reconciliation.

The story of *The Reader* is simple on the page, conceived, it seems, with the clarity of the fable. But once examined, its meanings become more complex. In the mid-1950s, a 15-year-old boy in a German provincial town, Michael Berg, is given a sexual initiation by an older woman, whom he has met when he has fallen ill on the way home and to whom he reads aloud great works of world literature. Even at the time and with so little experience, Michael, out of his depth, can nevertheless feel that the relationship has an undertow which is not wholly usual. Without warning, Hanna disappears from his life. Some years later, when, as an undergraduate studying law, Michael attends a war-crimes trial in a town near Heidelberg, he is shocked to discover that one of the defendants is his one-time lover. Hanna has worked as a guard in a concentration camp. On the subsequent death marches, she has committed a shocking war crime. But disturbingly, as the trial proceeds Michael realises he is in possession of evidence about her which, if he were to reveal it, would serve at least to mitigate Hanna's sentence. Can be bring himself to help someone whom he has loved but who he feels has betrayed him? Worse, what duty does he have towards someone who has done so many terrible things?

It's clear the moment you finish the novel that in no sense can it be seen as a book about forgiveness. On the contrary, Schlink makes it plain, both in his writing and in private conversation, that no writer of whatever background, portraying the crimes of the German people, has the moral right to extend to his characters any possibility of redemption. For that reason, it is immediately obvious to anyone whose unlikely response to the book is to want to make a film of it that they will be facing an unusual challenge. The conventional Hollywood narrative always ends in the hero coming to some understanding of his own flaws. Uplift, you may say, is built into the contract. But Hanna Schmidt, at the author's own insistence, reaches no real understanding of what she has done. You may even argue that no understanding of such extreme crimes is even possible. How, then, was anyone to embark on a movie in which one of the two principal characters essentially learns nothing?

Perhaps it was a mark of my stubbornness that I wanted to write the screenplay of *The Reader* precisely because I knew the task would be so unusual. More charitably, you could say that even by the time I read the book ten years ago, I was already, like so many contemporary cinemagoers, weary of genre pictures. Much as I still loved going to the cinema, I could no longer endure films which followed formulae the audience already recognized. For me, *Schindler's List* had represented a brilliant high-water-mark. I saw it once and never saw it again, because it achieved so completely what Godard had thought unachievable. It did justice to the sufferings of its subjects. It was both unnecessary and impossible to attempt to do it better. What excited me was the prospect of attempting its opposite. We would try to examine the same events but from the point of view of the perpetrators and of their descendants.

It isn't possible in the course of a short introduction to give any idea of just how tortured the path has been from reading the novel to finally sitting in front of a fresh-struck print of the film. All films are hard, but this one was harder than most, and as it turned out, crueller. The rights to the book had been sold on publication to the British filmmaker Anthony Minghella and his American partner Sydney Pollack, who together had formed a benign organization called Mirage which existed both to offer companionable help to fellow filmmakers, and for Sydney and Anthony to develop their own projects. However much I badgered Anthony to be allowed to write a screenplay, it was his firm intention to write and direct the film himself. It was only eight years later in the autumn of 2006 that Anthony finally rang the director Stephen Daldry to admit defeat. He would never be able to find time among his numerous commitments to get round to *The Reader*. He felt bad that he had not been able to fulfil his promise to the author of the book to make the film. So Stephen and I would therefore be allowed to go ahead, but on one condition. We must deliver the film within one calendar year of being granted the rights.

No one at that point could have foreseen the extraordinary series of misfortunes which soon overtook us. Some time after the start of filming, we lost our original leading lady, happily to pregnancy. So the shoot was first delayed and then suspended. During this hiatus, we worked again with Sydney and Anthony, two producers who made an interesting contrast—Anthony discursive, generous, professorial, like a popular teacher at a good university; Sydney quieter, more decisive, everyone's favourite acting coach, keen always to address the fundamental problems which on close examination can make the book seem so mysterious. Time and again, Sydney would draw us back to the question : What exactly is the metaphor of reading in the film? What is the function of literature?

During these relaxed meetings we talked with a collegiate ease which, in my experience, is pretty rare in modern Hollywood. Never once did Stephen and I feel we were working 'for' Sydney and Anthony. Rather, we were four collaborators on a film which fascinated us equally. So it was a loss beyond measure when both our producers died in the space of two months. We had long known Sydney was ill, dealing with cancer with characteristic grace and dispatch. But Anthony's death was out of the blue. I'd just sent him some notes on a scene I'd re-written. I'd got his reply. A few days later he was dead. Anthony was 54.

In the middle of these tragedies, somehow the film got made. There were two factors working in its favour. First, there was the skill and resilience of Stephen Daldry, onto whose shoulders the burden of the film at once fell. But second, and just as important, there was the steadfast excellence of the largely German cast and crew, led by Kate Winslet and Ralph Fiennes, and spotted with some of the greatest actors from the German theatre. At the outset, Stephen and I had felt like interlopers, daring to arrive in Berlin to address a subject which, you might think, our hosts knew far more intimately than we. The extraordinary scrupulousness of Stephen's historical research, the stunning accuracy of his reconstructions was more than a defensive gesture from a film-

The Reader

INT. MICHAEL'S APARTMENT. BERLIN. DAY. CREDITS

1995. A modern apartment, all cool and glass. MICHAEL BERG is preparing breakfast, laying the table for two. He is 51, dark-haired, saturnine. He is doing everything with deliberate quietness, taking the occasional glance towards the bedroom to check he's not making too much noise. He is boiling an egg, which he takes out of boiling water and puts on a sparkling clean plate.

MICHAEL puts the yolk-stained egg-cup and plate into the sink, his breakfast eaten, then, as noiseless as he can, turns on the tap to run water. The bedroom door opens, and BRIGITTE comes out, naked. She's attractive, younger. The credits end.

                    BRIGITTE
          You didn't wake me.

                    MICHAEL
          You were sleeping.

                    BRIGITTE
          You let me sleep because you can't bear to have
          breakfast with me.

It's half-serious. MICHAEL doesn't react.

                    MICHAEL
          Nothing could be further from the truth. I boiled
          you an egg. See?

MICHAEL produces a second boiled egg in a cup, seemingly from nowhere, like a magician, and puts it on the table.

> MICHAEL
>
> I'd hardly have boiled you an egg if I didn't want
> to see you. Tea or coffee?

BRIGITTE has reappeared from the bedroom, now in a dressing gown. She's still half-serious.

> BRIGITTE
>
> Does any woman ever stay long enough to find
> out what the hell goes on in your head?

MICHAEL smiles to himself.

> BRIGITTE
>
> What are you doing tonight?

> MICHAEL
>
> I'm seeing my daughter.

> BRIGITTE
>
> Your daughter? You've kept very quiet about her.

> MICHAEL
>
> Have I? She's been abroad for a year. Did you say
> tea?

INT. MICHAEL'S APARTMENT. BERLIN. DAY

MICHAEL kisses BRIGITTE on the cheek as she departs.

> BRIGITTE
>
> I'm going. Give my love to your daughter.

He closes the door, then turns to the open door of the bedroom. He looks at the mess of last night's love-making. Then he goes to the window and looks out. A yellow U-Bahn goes by.

INT. TRAM. DAY.

December 1958. MICHAEL, now 15, is sitting on a tram. He is in a well-cut suit he's inherited, ill-fitting, with two-tone shoes and tangled mop of hair. Sweat breaks out all over his face. A WOMAN is staring at him. He's plainly feeling ill.

INT. MICHAEL'S APARTMENT. DAY

1995. MICHAEL stands at the window, looking out.

INT. TRAM. DAY

1958. Impulsively, MICHAEL gets up, rings the bell and gets off at the next stop.

INT. MICHAEL'S APARTMENT. DAY

1995. MICHAEL closes the window.

EXT. BANHOFSTRASSE. DAY

1958. It has come onto rain. MICHAEL is walking along the street, looking more and more sickly. There is an archway leading to a courtyard, and impulsively, he darts inside to get out of the rain. He begins to vomit. Opposite him is a wood workshop open to the yard. A uniformed TRAM CONDUCTRESS walks past.

MICHAEL'S body is turned away, his face invisible, his hand over his mouth. She puts down her ticket machine on the pavement and seizes him by the arm.

                    HANNA
        Hey. Hey!

HANNA SCHMITZ has ash-blonde hair and is in her mid-thirties. She disappears. He's sick again. She reappears with a bucket of water to sluice down the pavement. She wipes his face down with a wet cloth. Then she fills another bucket.

                    HANNA
        Hey, kid. Hey.

                    MICHAEL
        I'm sorry. I'm sorry.

Effortlessly, HANNA takes MICHAEL in her arms. She holds his head against her breasts. MICHAEL buries himself and slowly he stops sobbing. Then he lifts his head.

                    HANNA
        Where do you live?

EXT. STREET. DAY

HANNA and MICHAEL walk at a fair pace along a street, dotted with the scaffolding of new building. HANNA is carrying his satchel, she is pulling him by the arm.

EXT. BLUMENSTRASSE. DAY

They come up the road. It is now snowing. MICHAEL stops outside his block, as if nervous she might come in.

MICHAEL

It's here. I'll be fine now. Thank you.

HANNA

Look after yourself.

MICHAEL smiles "Thank you" and goes in. HANNA is left alone. She looks round, frowning, then sets off, stopping uncertainly at the crossroads to check for the way she came. MICHAEL turns and watches, curious at her indecision.

INT. BERG APARTMENT. BLUMENSTRASSE. NIGHT

CARLA BERG is at the stove in the kitchen. She takes dinner through for the BERG family, at a round table in a traditional apartment, under a five-candled brass chandelier.

MICHAEL'S father, PETER, is a balding, abstracted man, eating in oppressive silence. Next to him, his older brother THOMAS, 18, his older sister, ANGELA, and his younger sister, EMILY. MICHAEL has his book in front of him, not touching his food.

CARLA

I'm worried about him. He looks terrible.

PETER

The boy's saying he doesn't need a doctor.

EMILY

He does.

MICHAEL

I don't need a doctor.

PETER

Good then.

CARLA looks reproachful.

> CARLA
>
> Peter.

> PETER
>
> We're not going to argue about this. People have
> to take responsibility for their own lives.

INT. BEDROOM. BERG APARTMENT. DAY

MICHAEL is lying in a single bed, his face is violently inflamed. CARLA is with the DOCTOR, a much older man.

> DOCTOR
>
> Remind me, how old are you now?

> CARLA
>
> Michael's fifteen.

> DOCTOR
>
> It's scarlet fever. He'll be in bed for several
> months. At least.

MICHAEL turns into the pillow, a wet patch beneath his head. Delusional with fever, he senses a presence at the door. He turns. It's EMILY. But at once CARLA's arm pulls her away.

> CARLA
>
> Keep away. He's contagious.

They vanish. The door closes. In the corridor the DOCTOR is heard.

> DOCTOR
>
> Burn the sheets. Complete isolation. And three
> months is the minimum.

INT & EXT. BERG APARTMENT. DAY

1959. A sunny day in March. MICHAEL's bed has been moved beside open windows so he can profit from the weak sun. He is sitting up, working on his stamp collection. CARLA is moving round behind him, tidying the room.

> CARLA
>
> How are you feeling?

> MICHAEL
>
> Better. By the way, I meant to tell you, the day I got ill . . . a woman helped me. A woman in the street.

> CARLA
>
> She helped you?

> MICHAEL
>
> Yes. She brought me home.

> CARLA
>
> Do you have her address?

EXT. BANHOFSTRASSE. DAY

MICHAEL is standing holding a small bunch of flowers. He is looking puzzled at a row of bells with numbers only. The woodyard is busy. WORKMEN come out of the building.

INT. STAIRS & LANDING. BANHOFSTRASSE. DAY

MICHAEL comes up the stairwell, once grand, now in decay—green linoleum and faded red paint. The sound of a sentimental song at the open door of a small apartment. Inside, HANNA is ironing in a sleeveless smock, blue with red flowers. Her hair is fastened in a clip. She looks at him a moment.

> HANNA
>
> Come in.

INT. HANNA'S APARTMENT. DAY

The flat is without decoration, an enfilade of small rooms. A stove, a sink, a tub, a boiler, a table, a few wooden chairs. There is no window, just a balcony door to let light into the room. HANNA carries on ironing.

> MICHAEL
>
> I brought you these flowers. To say thank you.

> HANNA
>
> Put them down there.

MICHAEL puts them beside the sink. HANNA has a blanket and a cloth over the table: nothing disturbs her rhythm, as she irons one piece of laundry after another, then folds it and puts it over one of the chairs.

> MICHAEL
>
> I would have come earlier, but I've been in bed for
> three months.

> HANNA
>
> You're better now?

> MICHAEL
>
> Thank you.

> HANNA
>
> Have you always been weak?

> MICHAEL

Oh no. I'd never been ill before. It's incredibly
boring. There's nothing to do. I couldn't even be
bothered to read.

HANNA carries on ironing. He is becoming as comfortable with the silence
as she is. She starts ironing a pair of knickers. He watches her bare arms moving back and forth. She looks broad-planed, strong. She is at peace with being watched. She puts one pair of knickers down, then does another. Then
she upends the iron.

> HANNA

I have to go to work. I'll walk with you. Wait in
the hall while I change.

MICHAEL goes out into the hall. The kitchen door is slightly open. HANNA
takes off her smock and stands in a green slip. Her stockings are hanging over
the back of a chair.

She picks one up, rolls it, smooths it up over her calf and knee, then attaches
it to her suspender. She reaches for the other. The flesh is bare between her
legs. MICHAEL watches, riveted. HANNA seems oblivious. But as she is
about to put the second stocking on, she looks at him. She drops her dress,
and straightens, holding her stare. In response, he blushes, then panics and
runs out of the flat. The door slams.

•

INT. STAIRS. DAY

MICHAEL runs down the stairs in terror and shame, and out the front door.

EXT. COURTYARD. DAY

The WORKMEN look up, curious, as MICHAEL flies by, slamming the
outer door.

9

INT. BEDROOM. DAWN

MICHAEL is lying in bed. He looks up at the sound of a tram going by outside.

EXT. STREET. DAWN

The tram making its way along the quiet street.

INT. BEDROOM. DAWN

MICHAEL gets out of bed and quickly gets dressed.

INT. TRAM. DAY

MICHAEL, reading a book, watches unobserved, fascinated as HANNA collects tickets. She calls out the name of the next stop. She doesn't see him as she works.

EXT. BANHOFSTRASSE. DAY

MICHAEL is standing on the other side of the street from HANNA'S court-yard. He is in two minds about whether to go in. The WOODWORKERS are loading a van. He waits for them to finish before he slips in through the archway, making his way to the stairs.

INT. LANDING. HANNA'S APARTMENT. DAY

MICHAEL is sitting on the steps of the first landing. Then, as if from no-where, HANNA is suddenly standing behind him, in uniform, carrying a box of coal in one hand, a scuttle in the other. She looks tired but not surprised to see him.

> HANNA
>
> There are two more buckets downstairs. You can
> fill them and bring them up.

HANNA walks straight past him. For a moment he tenses as if there might be some contact. But she goes by.

INT. CELLAR. DAY

MICHAEL opens the door. He turns on a dim light. There is a flight of wooden stairs into the murk of a huge pile of coke, poured in from the street. He goes down to the bottom and picks up a bucket. He digs into the coke, and at once it comes tumbling down on him in a cloud of dust.

INT. HANNA'S APARTMENT. DAY

HANNA is at the kitchen table, drinking a glass of milk. She has taken off her jacket and loosened her tie. MICHAEL comes in with the two buckets of coal, his face and clothes filthy. She roars with laughter, full-throated.

> HANNA
>
> You look ridiculous, look at you, kid.

MICHAEL sees himself in the mirror, but she has already got up, going towards the tub in the corner of the kitchen.

> HANNA
>
> You can't go home like that. Give me your clothes,
> I'll run you a bath.

HANNA opens the tap. There's a boiler, and steaming hot water comes out. MICHAEL takes off his sweater, then stops.

> HANNA
>
> What, do you always take a bath in your trousers?

HANNA takes his sweater and goes to open the balcony door. He undresses. She puts his sweater on the balcony rail.

> HANNA
>
> It's all right, I won't look.

On the contrary, she turns and walks straight towards him. MICHAEL is naked. HANNA takes his clothes from the chair. He gets into the bath. She goes to the balcony. In the bath, he submerges himself. HANNA goes out and shakes his clothes out in the open air.

When he comes up from under the water, she is laying his clothes back on the chair. She picks up the shampoo and hands it to him.

> HANNA
>
> Wash your hair, I'll get you a towel.

MICHAEL washes his hair, then submerges again. When he comes back up, HANNA is holding out a large towel. He gets out, turning away to hide his erection. From behind, she wraps his body and rubs him dry. Then she lets the towel fall. She puts her body against his back, and he realises she's naked. He turns and faces her.

> HANNA
>
> So. That's why you came back.

MICHAEL looks at her, awed.

> MICHAEL
>
> You're so incredibly beautiful.

HANNA

Now, kid, you know that's not true.

At once she puts her arms round him and they kiss. MICHAEL goes down
onto the floor, HANNA on top of him. All the time, she's staring into his
eyes. He can't take it. He closes his eyes and, about to come, begins to
scream. She puts her hand over his mouth to smother the noise.

INT. DINING ROOM. BERG APARTMENT. NIGHT

The family is half-way through their meal. MICHAEL is sitting watching
them eat, thinking about his lovemaking with HANNA.

PETER

You've inconvenienced your mother.

MICHAEL

How many more times? I've said I'm sorry.

PETER

You scared her.

MICHAEL

It's hardly my fault, I got lost, that's all. That's
why I was late. Can I have some more?

He reaches for more stew. THOMAS goes on eating, a look of contempt on
his face, too superior to engage in this.

EMILY

How can anyone get lost in their own hometown?

MICHAEL

The doctor told me I had to take walks.

EMILY

So?

MICHAEL

I meant to head for the castle; I ended up at the
sports field.

EMILY

They're in opposite directions.

MICHAEL

It's none of your business.

EMILY

He's lying.

CARLA

He's not lying. Michael never lies.

CARLA smiles benignly. EMILY knows she's right. They all eat on for a few
moments.

MICHAEL

Dad, I've decided, I want to go back to school
tomorrow.

CARLA

The doctor says you need another three weeks.

MICHAEL

Well, I'm going.

CARLA

Peter?

PETER
If he wants to go back, then he must.

MICHAEL can't breathe, as if some decisive moment in his life has been reached. PETER is looking at him, seeming to know what's going on.

EXT. SCHOOL. DAY

A massive brownstone building. The whole SCHOOL is coming out, but MICHAEL is first, in a desperate hurry, waving good-bye to his friends and running quickly away.

INT. STAIRS & LANDING. BANHOFSTRASSE. DAY

MICHAEL comes quickly up the stairs. The door of HANNA'S apartment is ajar. He pushes it open.

INT. HANNA'S APARTMENT. DAY

HANNA is at the sink. MICHAEL comes in, precipitate, tearing off his clothes and embracing her at the same time. He drops his trousers and lifts her onto the sink. He comes in about twenty seconds. He stands, sweating.

HANNA
All right, kid, it's not just about you.

INT. HANNA'S APARTMENT. DAY

They are on the bed. He is lying underneath her. HANNA leads his hands to her face, then down her body. She begins to move, and in response, he moves too. He watches awed as she comes.

15

INT. HANNA'S APARTMENT. DAY

HANNA has fallen asleep on MICHAEL'S chest. He is awake, looking at the birthmark on her left shoulder. The sound of the wood yard below. He kisses the birthmark. She stirs.

MICHAEL
What's your name?

She opens her eyes. A look of suspicion.

HANNA
What?

MICHAEL
Your name.

HANNA
Why do you want to know?

MICHAEL
I've been here three times. You haven't told me your name.

MICHAEL waits a moment.

HANNA
It's Hanna. What's yours, kid?

MICHAEL
Michael.

HANNA
Michael. Hmm. So I'm with a Michael.

HANNA smiles, as if there were something funny about it.

MICHAEL
Hanna.

INT. CLASSROOM. SCHOOL. DAY

A TEACHER, in his sixties, has scrawled the words "Odysseus," "Hamlet" and "Faust" on the blackboard. The class of BOYS is attentive. Next to him, his friend HOLGER SCHLUTER. Across the way, RUDOLF.

> TEACHER
> The notion of secrecy is central to Western liter-
> ature. You may say the whole idea of character in
> fiction is defined by people holding specific infor-
> mation which for various reasons—sometimes
> perverse, sometimes noble—they are determined
> not to disclose.

MICHAEL looks content. The bell goes.

INT. CORRIDOR. SCHOOL. DAY

The BOYS come pouring out cheerfully into the corridor and head to the next classroom. MICHAEL'S demeanour has changed. There's a knowing-ness, a swagger, a confidence which is new. MICHAEL lingers for a moment, then slopes off in the opposite direction, alone.

EXT. SCHOOL. DAY

MICHAEL comes out the back door of the school, unobserved, climbs over the railings and starts to run down the street.

INT. HANNA'S APARTMENT. EVENING

Later. Dark. MICHAEL is almost asleep, HANNA awake.

HANNA

You never tell me what you've been studying.

MICHAEL

Studying?

HANNA

At school. Do you learn languages?

MICHAEL

Yes.

HANNA

What languages?

MICHAEL

Latin.

HANNA

Say something in Latin.

MICHAEL

Oh . . .

MICHAEL thinks a moment.

MICHAEL

Quo, quo scelesti ruitis? Aut cur dexteris aptan-
tur enses conditi?

MICHAEL smiles slightly.

MICHAEL

It's Horace.

18

HANNA

It's wonderful.

MICHAEL

Do you want some Greek?

MICHAEL grins, pleased to be able to do something. He goes and gets his
satchel. HANNA turns on a light.

MICHAEL

Oi men ippeon stroton oi de pesedon oi da naon
phais epi gan malainan emmenai kalliston, ego
de ken otto tis eratai.

HANNA

It's beautiful.

MICHAEL

How can you tell? How do you know when you've
no idea what it means?

HANNA looks at him a moment.

HANNA

What about in German?

MICHAEL

In German?

HANNA

Do you have anything?

MICHAEL

Well, I'm writing an essay. It's about a play. By a
writer called Gotthold Ephraim Lessing. Perhaps
you've heard of him?

HANNA makes no reaction.

> MICHAEL

The play's called *Emilia Galotti*.

> HANNA

Have you got it?

MICHAEL reaches down to the satchel and pulls out a book.

> MICHAEL

Here. You can read it.

> HANNA

I'd rather listen to you.

There is a silence as MICHAEL absorbs the idea.

> MICHAEL

All right. I'm not very good.

MICHAEL grins, embarrassed, then opens the book.

> MICHAEL

Act One. Scene One. The setting: one of the
prince's chambers. Prince: "Complaints, nothing
but complaints, petitions, nothing but petitions.
For goodness' sake, just imagine that people ac-
tually envy us."

INT. KITCHEN. NIGHT

Later. They are in the bath together. HANNA takes a piece of soap
and runs it lovingly down his cheek. Then she passes the soap across his
stomach.

> HANNA

You're good at it, aren't you?

> MICHAEL

Good at what?

> HANNA

Reading.

He smiles.

> HANNA

Why are you smiling?

> MICHAEL

Because I didn't think I was good at anything.

INT. GYMNASIUM. DAY

MICHAEL is playing handball with terrific physical confidence. A couple of bruising physical encounters. HOLGER, RUDOLF and MICHAEL all laugh. The whistle blows. Game over.

EXT. TRAM. DAWN

An empty tram moving through the eerie early-morning streets. MICHAEL appears walking alongside it and gets on.

INT. TRAM. DAWN

MICHAEL is sitting in the second carriage. He looks up. The CONDUC-TRESS is HANNA. At first, she does not notice him. MICHAEL watches, waiting to be noticed. She turns round and looks at him. He smiles in greeting, but she makes no acknowledgement at all. She turns away. He frowns, bewildered.

EXT. TRAM. DAY

The tram is heading out of town.

INT. TRAM. DAY

HANNA is now talking animatedly to the DRIVER. They are getting on very well, laughing together and chatting. MICHAEL is still by himself in the second carriage, looking foolish.

EXT. TRAM. DAY

The tram comes to a halt and PASSENGERS get on.

INT. TRAM. DAY

HANNA is now in the busy second carriage, collecting tickets. MICHAEL looks up expectantly. But as he holds up his ticket, HANNA makes no re-action except to clip it. She turns away without speaking. The tram comes to a halt again, and MICHAEL, humiliated, bolts for the door.

EXT. ROAD. DAY

MICHAEL watches the tram disappear up the hill. He looks around, lost, in the middle of nowhere. A tractor goes by, WORKERS heading to the fields. MICHAEL sets off to walk back to town.

INT. LANDING. HANNA'S APARTMENT. DAY

MICHAEL is on the stairs as HANNA comes up, in her uniform.

MICHAEL

What was all that about?

HANNA lets herself in, saying nothing.

INT. HANNA'S APARTMENT. DAY

HANNA has gone in to put down her things at the kitchen table. MICHAEL follows, desperate.

MICHAEL

I got up—at 4:30—specially—it's the first day of the holidays, I'd been planning to surprise you—

HANNA

Poor little baby. Got up at four thirty—and on your holidays, too.

MICHAEL

What is this? I was on your tram! You totally ignored me! What do you think I was doing? Why the hell do you think I was there?

MICHAEL has yelled in desperation. HANNA looks him straight in the eye.

HANNA

I haven't the slightest idea. And what you do is your business not mine.

HANNA turns and moves away.

HANNA

And if you wanted to speak to me, I was in the first carriage. So why did you sit in the second?

23

HANNA goes to run a bath.

> HANNA
>
> And now, thanks very much, I've been working,
> I need a bath. Get out, I'd like to be by myself.

> MICHAEL
>
> I didn't mean to upset you.

> HANNA
>
> You don't have the power to upset me. You don't
> matter enough to upset me.

She takes off her clothes to get in. As soon as she does, he gets up and goes into the other room. He sits by himself, miserable. He hears her, bathing. Then he finally gets up and goes back in. She is still in the bath.

> MICHAEL
>
> I don't know what to say. I've never been with a
> woman. We've been together four weeks and I
> can't live without you. I can't. Even the thought
> of it kills me.

HANNA looks at him thoughtfully.

> MICHAEL
>
> I sat in the second carriage because I thought you
> might kiss me.

> HANNA
>
> Kid, you thought we could make love in a tram?

They smile. But MICHAEL has a more urgent question.

> MICHAEL
>
> Is it true what you said? That I don't matter to you?

In the bath, she shakes her head.

> MICHAEL
>
> Do you forgive me?

She nods.

> MICHAEL
>
> Do you love me?

She looks at him. Then she nods.

INT. BEDROOM. HANNA'S APARTMENT. DAY

MICHAEL is sitting on the side of the bed. HANNA comes in, wrapped in a towel.

> HANNA
>
> Do you have a book?

> MICHAEL
>
> Oh. Well, I do. I took something with me this morning.

> HANNA
>
> What is it?

> MICHAEL
>
> It's another play.

MICHAEL gets it out of his pocket. HANNA has lain down on the bed, completely content.

> HANNA
>
> We're changing the order we do things. Read to me first, kid. Then we make love.

MICHAEL sits at the foot of the bed and starts to read.

> MICHAEL
> *Intrigue and Love,* a play by Friedrich Schiller . . .

INT. HANNA'S APARTMENT. DAY

HANNA is baking bread. MICHAEL is on a chair beside her with a book.

> MICHAEL
> *The Odyssey* by Homer.

> HANNA
> What's an odyssey?

> MICHAEL
> It's a journey. He sets out on a journey.

He starts to read.

> MICHAEL
> "Sing to me of the Man, Muse, the man of twists
> and turns
> Driven time and again off course, once he had
> plundered
> The hallowed heights of Troy.
> Many cities of men he saw and learned their minds,
> Many pains he suffered, heartsick at the open sea,
> Fighting to save his life and bring his comrades
> home . . ."

INT. HANNA'S APARTMENT. EVENING

HANNA is in the bath. MICHAEL is reading her a Shakespeare sonnet.

MICHAEL

"And we will some new pleasures prove of golden
sands and crystal brooks, with silken lights and
silver hooks . . ."

HANNA

Come here.

She pulls him into the bath.

INT. HANNA'S APARTMENT. NIGHT

HANNA is sewing. MICHAEL is reading *Huckleberry Finn.*

MICHAEL

"I poked into the place aways and encountered a
little open patch as big as a bedroom, all hung
around with vines and found a man lying there
asleep, and by Jinks it was my old Jim . . ."

He starts acting out Jim, and the two of them collapse laughing.

INT. HANNA'S APARTMENT. DAY

MICHAEL is at the bottom of the bed. HANNA is lying inside. He is reading *Lady Chatterley's Lover.*

MICHAEL

"Lady Chatterley felt his naked flesh against her
as he came into her. For a moment he was still inside her . . ."

HANNA

This is disgusting. Where did you get this?

MICHAEL

I borrowed it from someone at school.

HANNA

You should be ashamed. Go on.

INT. HANNA'S APARTMENT. EVENING

MICHAEL reads *Tintin* to HANNA, who is lying on the bed. They are both
looking at the pictures.

MICHAEL

"'Blistering Barnacles and a thundering typhoon.
It is water.' 'But what on earth did you expect it
to be?'"

HANNA

Whisky.

MICHAEL

"Whisky! By thunder, whisky. 'Whisky? Come
now captain, you can't be serious.'"

HANNA

All right, kid, that's enough for today.

They fall back onto the bed.

MICHAEL

I was wondering, do you think you could get some
time off? Maybe we could go for a trip.

HANNA

What sort of trip?

MICHAEL

I'd love to go bicycling. Just for two days.

28

MICHAEL reaches for a book.

> MICHAEL
> I've got a guidebook. I've worked out the route.
> Look, what do you think?

HANNA'S look is so faraway, she doesn't seem to hear the question. Silence. Then:

> HANNA
> I think you like planning, don't you?

She throws the book away and they begin to make love.

INT. BEDROOM. BERG APARTMENT. DAWN

First light. Dawn breaking outside the window. MICHAEL is working at his desk, the surface covered in stamps, his collection book open. He picks one with a pyramid on it and looks at it. Underneath, MICHAEL'S VOICE reading *Intrigue and Love* by Schiller.

> MICHAEL'S VOICE
> "I'm not frightened. I'm not frightened of any-
> thing. Why should I be? I welcome obstacles, be-
> cause they'll be like mountains I can fly over to
> be in your arms. The more I suffer, the more I'll
> love . . ."

INT & EXT. SHOP. DAY

Seen from outside, a shop full of stamps. MICHAEL and a STAMP DEALER with white hair and a moustache. MICHAEL is offering his pyramid stamp, his gestures becoming desperate as the STAMP DEALER shakes his head, clearly not giving him as much as he hopes. Then MICHAEL concedes, the

DEALER concedes, and a bunch of notes are handed across. MICHAEL runs exhilarated out into the street.

>   MICHAEL'S VOICE
> "Danger will only increase my love, it will sharpen
> it, it will give it spice. I'll be the only angel you
> need. On this arm, Luise, you will go dancing
> through life. You will leave life even more beau-
> tiful than you entered it. Heaven will take you
> back and look at you and say 'Only one thing can
> make a soul complete, and that thing is love.'"

EXT. HILL. DAY

HANNA and MICHAEL are whizzing down a hill together on bicycles. He has a rucksack. It's a rural paradise—hills on all sides, a gleaming river below, the sun shining brightly. She is wearing a blue dress.

EXT. CAFE. DAY

They come to a cafe and sit down outside. They pick up the menus on the table. A WAITRESS arrives.

>   WAITRESS
> So what would you like to have?

>   MICHAEL
> What are you having?

>   HANNA
> You order. I'll have what you have.

MICHAEL starts giving the order. Next to them is a group of BOY SCOUTS, who are laughing among themselves.

BOYS

There's sausages, sausages or sausages. Give it to
me, come on, give it here. Let me have a look. You
always have the same thing.

They all laugh. HANNA watches them nervously.

EXT. CAFE. DAY

The meal finished, MICHAEL is alone, paying the bill.

WAITRESS

I hope your mother was happy.

MICHAEL

Thank you. She enjoyed her meal very much.

The WAITRESS goes. HANNA returns from inside. MICHAEL holds out
his arm to her, which she takes. They walk away towards their bikes. He is
smiling. MICHAEL looks round, then dares to reach across and kiss her on
the lips. The WAITRESS watches.

EXT. CHURCH. DAY

They get off their bikes at a small church. MICHAEL stops and gets out a
map and a guidebook.

MICHAEL

Here, let me show you where we're going.

HANNA

It's OK, kid. I don't want to know.

The sound of a choir from inside.

INT. CHURCH. DAY

MICHAEL and HANNA enter tentatively to find a choir rehearsing Bach.
It is a traditional German scene—whole families singing together at the al-
tar. HANNA is transported, entranced at the sound of the music. MICHAEL
watches.

EXT. RIVERSIDE. DAY

HANNA is in a river, the water up to her calves, her skirt tied round her
thighs. She is completely absorbed. Then she looks up, aware of being
watched. MICHAEL is sitting with a notebook.

                         HANNA
        What are you doing?

                         MICHAEL
        I'm writing a poem. About you.

                         HANNA
        Can I hear it?

                         MICHAEL
        It's not ready. I'll read it to you one day.

INT. MICHAEL'S APARTMENT. BERLIN. DAY

1995. MICHAEL, now 51, is standing by his desk. He opens a drawer.
He takes out the recognizable notebook. He opens its yellowing pages
and looks at the poetry. Then flips the pages, to some handwritten
lists—the words "Odyssey," "Schnitzler," "Chekhov," "Zweig," with
numbers beside them. MICHAEL flips it shut, puts it back and turns to
go out.

INT. STREET. DAY

MICHAEL leaves his apartment block. He gets into his black Mercedes.

INT. CAR. DAY

MICHAEL is listening on the radio to the same Bach music they heard in the church. He drives through the thriving modern city. Beyond, the huge cranes and gouged-out building sites of a city under construction.

EXT. STREET. DAY

MICHAEL swings his car into place. He gets out and heads across the road, prosperous, purposeful.

INT. LOBBY. COURTHOUSE. DAY

An ASSISTANT meets MICHAEL with his robe, which he pulls on as he walks quickly through an elaborate lobby. GERHARD BADE, also in his fifties, also robed, falls in step.

> GERHARD
> You all right, Michael?

> MICHAEL
> I'm fine.

> GERHARD
> You'd better hurry. You know what she's like.

A robed ASSISTANT is waiting outside the door with documents he hands to MICHAEL. They all go in.

INT. COURTROOM. DAY

MICHAEL joins his CLIENT, just seconds before the FEMALE JUDGE comes in and everyone stands. Silence. The JUDGE looks at MICHAEL disapprovingly, sensing his lateness. Everyone sits. MICHAEL sits, thinking back.

INT. STAIRWAY. SCHOOL. DAY

1958. A sheriff's posse of sixteen-year-old GIRLS, come laughing, blushing towards the classroom. One of them is talking excitedly to the other.

> SOPHIE
> I'm just going to pretend I've been here for years,
> I'm not going to behave in any special way.

> GIRL
> You just wait. You wait and see.

They smile together and head for the classroom.

INT. SCHOOL. DAY

The BOYS are already in place, dotted round, as the GIRLS come in. There are cries of "Here they come." Then the TEACHER comes in.

> TEACHER
> Good morning, ladies. Gentlemen, please wel-
> come your new fellow-students, treat them with
> courtesy, please.

Not far from MICHAEL, a GIRL sits across the aisle, virginal, with brown hair, brown summer skin.

                         SOPHIE
          Hello. My name's Sophie.

                        MICHAEL
          I'm Michael.

The TEACHER comes in. The class quietens.

INT. SCHOOL. DAY

Later. The TEACHER is in full flow. MICHAEL can't take his eyes off
SOPHIE.

                        TEACHER
          Everyone believes that Homer's subject is home-
          coming. In fact, *The Odyssey* is a book about a jour-
          ney. Home is a place you dream of, it's not a place
          you ever attain.

The TEACHER breaks off.

                        TEACHER
          Berg, I don't mean to distract you, but we're meant
          to studying Homer, not studying Sophia.

The whole class cracks up. MICHAEL blushes.

EXT. SWIMMING LAKE. DAY

MICHAEL is riveted as SOPHIE swims fast and lithe through the water.
Around him, YOUNG PEOPLE are lounging round on towels. It's the so-
cial centre. HOLGER and RUDOLF are rubbing their hair with towels as
SOPHIE approaches.

                           35

                                HOLGER

Michael, the water's fantastic.

                                MICHAEL

It's wonderful, isn't it?

                                HOLGER

Wonderful. It's going to be a great summer.

MICHAEL looks across to where a group of AMERICANS are shouting and
playing a very loud game of volleyball.

                                HOLGER

Now the Americans have allowed us back in our
own lake.

                                SOPHIE

Why are they so loud?

                                HOLGER

You should see their stores. They have everything.

                                MICHAEL

Oh sure. Everything mankind could ever dream of.

                                SOPHIE

You don't like Americans?

                                MICHAEL

Just, it's more fun without them.

He looks SOPHIE straight in the eye. There is a sudden silence, MICHAEL
looking straight at SOPHIE. SOPHIE looks down. Then MICHAEL moves
slightly to pack up his stuff.

                                SOPHIE

Why do you leave early?

HOLGER

He always leaves early.

EXT. BANHOFSTRASSE. DAY

MICHAEL is cycling back towards town, a smile on his face.

INT. HANNA'S APARTMENT. DAY

MICHAEL flies up the stairs, then goes in. HANNA is sitting, sewing. He kisses her on the cheek as he gets out a book.

MICHAEL

I'm sorry I'm late. I was held up at school.

At once he sits down opposite her. A ritual.

MICHAEL

The Lady with the Little Dog. By Anton Chekhov.

HANNA looks, seeing right through him.

MICHAEL

"The talk was that a new face had appeared on the promenade, a lady with a little dog."

INT. GARAGE. DAY

A huge tram-shed full of empty trams. HANNA is at the end of the garage, talking to the SUPERVISOR, a large man in his fifties.

SUPERVISOR

Schmitz, one moment. We've got good news for you. Your work is good, we're going to promote you. To work with me in the office. It's more money. Congratulations.

He moves away. HANNA looks distraught.

EXT. SWIMMING LAKE. DAY

MICHAEL is watching SOPHIE swimming, a look of anxiety in his eye, when HOLGER touches his shoulder.

> HOLGER
> Get a move on, we're leaving early today.

> MICHAEL
> Why? What for?

> HOLGER
> We're going back to Sophie's. It's your birthday.
> We're giving you a party.

HOLGER and RUDOLF disappear to get dressed. SOPHIE appears in her swimming costume.

> SOPHIE
> Come on, it's a surprise. We thought you'd like it.
> We've been planning it for weeks.

> MICHAEL
> I'm sorry. Really. I promised someone I'd do something else.

The others are furious with him. They all go off.

EXT. STREET. DAY

MICHAEL is cycling towards HANNA'S apartment, his hair wet from the lake, looking equally unhappy.

INT. HANNA'S APARTMENT. DAY

HANNA is sitting unhappily as MICHAEL reads to her. They are both in a bad mood.

> HANNA
>
> Oh kid, kid. Stop.

> MICHAEL
>
> What's wrong?

> HANNA
>
> Nothing's wrong. It's nothing.

HANNA just shrugs. She goes and sits at the table to drink tea. MICHAEL is irritated.

> MICHAEL
>
> You never ask, you never bother to ask how I am.

> HANNA
>
> You never say.

> MICHAEL
>
> It just happens to be my birthday. It's my birthday, that's all. In fact, you've never even asked when it is.

> HANNA
>
> Look, if you want a fight, kid . . .

> MICHAEL
>
> No, I don't want a fight. What's wrong with you?

> HANNA
>
> What business is it of yours?

39

She has snapped at him, razor-like.

> MICHAEL
>
> It's always on your terms. Everything. We do what
> you want. It's always what you want. My friends
> were giving me a party!

> HANNA
>
> Well then, why are you here? Go back to your
> party. Isn't that what you want?

HANNA puts down her cup, angry. She goes into the bedroom and slams
the door. He sits, the magic of the day gone. He gets up and opens the bedroom door. HANNA is on the bed.

> MICHAEL
>
> And it's always me that has to apologize.

Silence. HANNA lets time go by. Then:

> HANNA
>
> You don't have to apologize. No one *has* to apol-
> ogize. No one can make you.

HANNA reaches for a book from beside the bed. She throws it down on
the cover.

> HANNA
>
> *War and Peace*, kid.

INT. HANNA'S APARTMENT. DAY

HANNA is on the edge of the bath, running water. She has a pale blue flow-
ered smock. She is running with sweat. The smock sticks to her. MICHAEL

gets out a book. HANNA drops lavender oil into the bath. MICHAEL stands in the bath and she washes his body.

INT. HANNA'S APARTMENT. DAY

They are making love on the bed. It's intense. At one point she moves on top of him. She holds his head between her hands, as if she would crush the life out of him. Then she lets go.

INT. HANNA'S APARTMENT. DAY

They are both sweating, exhausted. She looks a moment.

> HANNA
> Now you must go back to your friends.

INT. HANNA'S APARTMENT. DAY

MICHAEL has gone. HANNA washes out milk bottles and empties them into the sink. Then she picks up her luggage and leaves the empty apartment.

EXT. SWIMMING LAKE. DAY

MICHAEL is sitting on the pier watching as HOLGER, RUDOLF and SOPHIE swim competitively out to a pontoon, then turn back, full of energy and high spirits. MICHAEL watches for a while, then suddenly he gets up and starts to run away from them all.

> SOPHIE
> Michael. You all right?

But MICHAEL is running away across the lakeside beach.

INT. LANDING & HANNA'S APARTMENT. DUSK

MICHAEL opens the door. He goes in. The apartment is emptied, the rented furniture in place, all trace of HANNA gone. He looks round. He looks at the empty bath, the tap above it. He opens the kitchen cupboards—some coffee, sugar, that's about it. He goes into the bedroom—the bed stripped bare. He lies down on the bed.

INT. HANNA'S APARTMENT. NIGHT

MICHAEL, lying on the bed, curled up, in his clothes, like a foetus, asleep.

INT. APARTMENT. DAY

The family at breakfast. MICHAEL slips quietly in the main door, trying to go to his room without being heard. EMILY runs to look.

> EMILY
>
> It's him.

Sheepishly, MICHAEL appears.

> CARLA
>
> Where were you last night? What happened?

> MICHAEL
>
> I stayed at a friend's.

> PETER
>
> Carla.

PETER looks. He seems to know exactly what's been going on.

> PETER
>
> Get the boy something to eat. I think we all knew
> you'd come back to us eventually.

EXT. SWIMMING LAKE. DUSK

MICHAEL is alone in the deserted pool. He is on the jetty. He takes off his clothes and slips into the water. Just his head, like a seal's, at one end, just out of the water, quite still.

INT. COURTHOUSE. NIGHT

1995. MICHAEL sitting alone, thinking back.

EXT. SWIMMING LAKE. DUSK

1958. The sun slants, and for a few seconds the water dazzles. He slips his head under.

INT. COURTHOUSE. DAY

1995. MICHAEL still sitting thoughtfully by himself in the empty court. Then he looks up. An ASSISTANT has appeared.

ASSISTANT

Mr. Berg. It is eight o'clock. Your daughter.

MICHAEL

Thank you.

He gets up.

INT. BRASSERIE. BERLIN. NIGHT

JULIA is already at the table in a chic, modern brasserie. She is a sympathetic young woman of around 23. MICHAEL approaches. When she sees him, she gets up.

JULIA

I was early.

MICHAEL leans in and kisses her on the cheek.

MICHAEL

Julia.

They're uneasy. She looks a moment, then they sit down.

MICHAEL

Welcome back.

INT. RESTAURANT. NIGHT

Later. They have eaten. They both have big glasses of red wine. It's more relaxed.

MICHAEL

So, how will you decide?

JULIA

I don't know. I'm happy back in Berlin, I suppose.

MICHAEL

You've seen your mother?

JULIA nods.

JULIA

I wanted to get away. There was nothing more to
it. It was Paris, but it could have been anywhere.

MICHAEL

Away from your parents?

44

JULIA doesn't answer.

> MICHAEL
>
> I'm aware I was difficult. I wasn't always open
> with you. I'm not open with anyone.

> JULIA
>
> I knew you were distant. I'd always assumed it
> was my fault.

> MICHAEL
>
> Julia. How wrong can you be?

JULIA colors, on the verge of tears. Then she looks away.

INT & EXT. CAR. NIGHT

They drive through the gleaming streets. It's been raining—Berlin is glistening. Their voices:

> MICHAEL
>
> I admit it now, I was nervous.

> JULIA
>
> I was nervous too. It's silly, isn't it?

> MICHAEL
>
> It is silly.

> JULIA
>
> Thank you for dinner.

> MICHAEL
>
> I'll see you very soon.

EXT. CAR. DAY

MICHAEL lets JULIA out, and is watching her safely to her door from the car.

> JULIA

Good night, Dad.

MICHAEL suddenly gets out himself.

> MICHAEL

Julia, wait. I want to ask you a favor.

> JULIA

What favor?

> MICHAEL

I want to take you on a trip. I want to show you something.

> JULIA

When?

> MICHAEL

Tomorrow, maybe. Can I pick you up in the car?

JULIA doesn't need to say anything.

> MICHAEL

At ten, say.

JULIA smiles.

> MICHAEL

Then good.

MICHAEL hugs her, his heart aching with love. JULIA goes into her place. MICHAEL is left standing still in the plaza outside, not moving. Underneath the sound of what follows, thirty years previously.

INT. LECTURE ROOM. HEIDELBERG LAW SCHOOL. DAY

1966. A WOMAN LECTURER has a class of about 75 STUDENTS. From their hair, their dress, it could only be the 1960s.

> LECTURER
> Those of you for the special seminar group on The Legal System in the Third Reich, please stay on in this room. Professor Rohl will be here in a moment.

Nearly all the STUDENTS leave, talking among themselves. Just eight are left, dotted around the huge room. MICHAEL is one of them, now 22, in a corduroy jacket and tie. There is a lull. MICHAEL looks round at the group of oddballs, then finds ROHL, distinguished, greying, is already in front of them.

> ROHL
> Well, we seem to be quite a small group. A small group and a select one. Clearly, this is going to be a unique seminar. Let me start by thanking those of you who've chosen to take part. Good for you. A reading list, gentlemen. Karl Jaspers, *The Question of German Guilt* . . .

A calm STUDENT with long hair smiles at MICHAEL. She looks like Francoise Hardy. She murmurs.

> MARTHE
> And ladies.

INT. STUDENT DIGS. NIGHT

MICHAEL is working alone at his desk, a light on. The door of his ex-
tremely modest student digs is open. MARTHE appears at the door,
silently. He looks up.

MARTHE

So this is where you are.

MICHAEL

Yes. Come in.

But neither of them moves. MARTHE just smiles from the door.

MARTHE

You take work seriously.

MICHAEL

Oh, I don't know.

MARTHE

You're rather a serious boy.

MARTHE shrugs slightly.

MICHAEL

It's how I was brought up. What about you? Are
you serious?

MARTHE

You're sure you want to work tonight?

MICHAEL

Well, I do. But I won't work every night.

MARTHE

See you tomorrow.

They smile at each other. She goes.

INT. TRAIN. DAY

The seminar group, long-haired, hippyish, is on the train: PROFESSOR
ROHL, with MARTHE, DIETER and a few others. MICHAEL catches
MARTHE'S eye. They smile. Then he opens the window, cheerful.

EXT. TOWN HALL. MANNHEIM. DAY

The STUDENTS are having a cigarette in front of the huge building. Two
black vans with barred windows come by, carrying prisoners. The first one
veers close to MICHAEL on the pavement, then disappears into the inner
courtyard. ROHL smiles at MICHAEL.

MICHAEL

Why all the police?

ROHL

They're worried about demonstrators.

MICHAEL

For or against?

ROHL

Both.

INT. TOWN HALL. DAY

A courtroom has been improvised inside the town hall. There are large
windows, with milky glass, down the left-hand side. As ROHL and the

STUDENTS arrive, the court is a melée of PHOTOGRAPHERS, LAW-
YERS and PUBLIC. The three JUDGES are already in place, next to six selected CITIZENS. MICHAEL and the others take places in the gallery.

CLERK

All photographers are now asked to leave.

The PHOTOGRAPHERS go.

JUDGE

The defendants, please.

From being noisy and chaotic, the court is now silent.

JUDGE

The first thing I'm going to do is hear motions
from each of the defendants' lawyers. They're going to be arguing that there's no reason to keep
the defendants in jail until the outcome of the
forthcoming trial.

DIETER grins at MICHAEL in anticipation.

JUDGE

I am going to take these cases one by one.

MICHAEL is leaning down to get stuff out of his briefcase, as MARTHE
shakes a pen, which isn't working.

MICHAEL

Do you want a pen?

MARTHE

I've got a pen.

So MICHAEL doesn't hear as the JUDGE speaks.

                            JUDGE

Hanna Schmitz.

There is a row of six DEFENDANTS. The fifth woman is HANNA, her hair
tied in a knot, her gaze fixedly into the middle distance, not looking towards
the SPECTATORS. She is wearing a grey dress with short sleeves. They all
sit, sideways to the gallery. HANNA rises to her feet. The words seem to
come very quietly, across a great distance.

                            JUDGE

Your name is Hanna Schmitz?

                            HANNA

Yes.

It is only when the JUDGE repeats the name that MICHAEL looks up, hear-
ing it for the first time.

                            JUDGE

Can you speak louder, please?

                            HANNA

My name is Hanna Schmitz.

MICHAEL is rigid, blank, just staring.

                            JUDGE

Thank you. You were born on October 21st,
1922?

                            HANNA

Yes.

                            JUDGE

At Hermannstadt. And you're now 43 years old?

HANNA

Yes.

JUDGE

You joined the SS in 1943?

HANNA

Yes.

JUDGE

What was your reason? What was your reason for joining?

HANNA doesn't answer.

JUDGE

You were working at the Siemens factory at the time?

HANNA

Yes.

JUDGE

You'd recently been offered a promotion. Why did you prefer to join the SS?

HANNA has a DEFENSE COUNSEL, a young man, beside her, who is about to get up. But the JUDGE forestalls him.

JUDGE

I'll rephrase my question. I'm trying to ascertain if she joined the SS freely. Of her own free will.

Everyone waits.

JUDGE

Well?

HANNA

I heard there were jobs.

JUDGE

Go on.

HANNA

I was working at Siemens when I heard the SS was
recruiting.

JUDGE

Did you know the kind of work you'd be expected
to do?

HANNA

They were looking for guards. I applied for a job.

MICHAEL is intent now, so are the STUDENTS beside him.

JUDGE

And you worked first at Auschwitz?

HANNA

Yes.

JUDGE

Until 1944. Then you were moved to a smaller
camp near Cracow?

HANNA

Yes.

ROHL leans in to MICHAEL.

> ROHL
>
> Are you OK?

> MICHAEL
>
> I'm fine.

> JUDGE
>
> You then helped move the prisoners west in the winter of 1944, in the so-called death marches?

INT. TRAIN. DAY

MICHAEL is hanging out of the window of the train, smoking a cigarette.

INT. TRAIN. DAY

MICHAEL sits down in his seat. ROHL moves to sit opposite him.

> ROHL
>
> So, what did you think?

> MICHAEL
>
> I don't know. It wasn't quite what I was expecting.

> ROHL
>
> Wasn't it? In what way? What were you expecting?

ROHL is looking at him. MICHAEL doesn't answer.

> DIETER
>
> I thought it was exciting.

ROHL

How so?

DIETER

Because we're not implicated.

ROHL

Aren't you? Good. So that's all right, then.

Everyone laughs.

MARTHE

No, but seriously, Dieter's right. My parents, I
can't even talk to them. I don't love them. How
could I? How could anyone love them? Because
they've told themselves so many lies, they can't remember the truth, let alone admit it. Isn't that
why we signed up for this seminar?

ROHL

I don't know. You tell me.

MARTHE

Speaking for myself.

ROHL

Michael?

MICHAEL

I'm not sure anymore.

ROHL is staring at him thoughtfully.

ROHL

What did your father do, Dieter?

DIETER

If you want to know, he was in the Waffen SS.

There are some smiles, but DIETER rides over the reaction.

DIETER

That's what I mean, that's what I'm saying. So were a million other Germans.

ROHL

That's exactly my point. That's why it's better not to pretend this is about justice. Forgive me, nor is it about getting into an emotional state. It has no purpose if it's just the young giving their parents a bad time.

There's a silence. That's clearly why some of them are there.

MARTHE

So what is it about? What do you think?

ROHL

Societies think they operate by something called morality. But they don't. They operate by something called law. You're not guilty of anything merely by working at Auschwitz. 8,000 people worked at Auschwitz. Precisely 19 have been convicted, and only 6 for murder. To prove murder you have to prove intent. That's the law. Remember, the question is never 'Was it wrong?' but 'Was it legal?' And not by our laws, no, by the laws at the time.

DIETER frowns, unhappy.

DIETER

But isn't that . . .

ROHL

What?

DIETER

Narrow?

ROHL

Yes. The law is narrow.

ROHL looks unapologetic.

ROHL

On the other hand, I suspect people who kill other
people tend to be aware that it's wrong.

INT. COURTROOM. MANNHEIM. DAY

ROHL is leaning forward, attentive. HANNA is standing, opposite the
JUDGE, who holds up a book called *MOTHER & DAUGHTER: A STORY
OF SURVIVAL*.

JUDGE

Miss Schmitz, you're familiar with this book . . .

HANNA

Yes . . .

JUDGE

Parts of it have already been read out in court. It's
an American publication, which has been trans-
lated. It's by a survivor, a prisoner who survived,
Ilana Mather . . .

HANNA

Yes, I know. I know Ilana Mather.

JUDGE

She was in the camp, wasn't she, when she was a child? She was with her mother.

The judge waits. HANNA seems arrogant, defiant.

JUDGE

In the book, she describes a selection process. At the end of the month's labor, every month, sixty inmates were selected. They were picked out to be sent from the satellite camp back to Auschwitz. That's right, isn't it?

HANNA

Yes, it's right.

JUDGE

And so far, each of your fellow defendants has specifically denied being part of that process. Now I'm going to ask you. Were you part of it?

HANNA

Yes.

There is a stir among the other DEFENDANTS and in the court. They start talking to their LAWYERS.

JUDGE

So you helped make the selection?

HANNA

Yes.

JUDGE

You admit that? Then tell me, how did that selection happen?

HANNA shrugs slightly, as though it were obvious.

HANNA

There were six guards, so we decided we'd choose
ten people each. That's how we did it—every
month. We'd all choose ten.

JUDGE

Are you saying your fellow defendants took part
in the process?

HANNA

We all did.

JUDGE

Even though they've denied it? But you admit it.
You're saying you took part in the process.

The other DEFENDANTS stir with animosity, but the JUDGE is intent,
following his own line.

JUDGE

Did you not realise you were sending these women
to their deaths?

He waits. HANNA nods slightly.

HANNA

Yes but there were new arrivals, new women were
arriving all the time, so of course we had to move
some of the old ones on.

JUDGE

I'm not sure you understand . . .

HANNA

We couldn't keep everyone. There wasn't room.

The JUDGE frowns, genuinely surprised that she doesn't seem to understand his point.

JUDGE

No, but what I'm saying: let me rephrase: to *make* room, you were picking women out and saying, 'You you and you have to be sent back to be killed.'

HANNA

Well, what would you have done?

HANNA is looking at the JUDGE—a perfectly straight question. MICHAEL smiles slightly, proud of her. Everyone in the court waits for the JUDGE to answer. Silence. ROHL is impassive. But HANNA follows her own thoughts. She quietly asks herself a question.

HANNA

So should I never have signed up at Siemens?

INT. LOBBY. TOWN HALL. DAY

MICHAEL is alone, smoking. On a bench, side by side, are two women. One is very small, dark, in her sixties. The other is composed, formidable, elegant, in her thirties. ROSE and ILANA MATHER. They look up, catching MICHAEL's eye. Then a CLERK leans in to the younger woman.

CLERK

Ms. Mather, they're ready for you now.

The two women go into the court. The door closes.

INT. LOBBY & COURTROOM. DAY

MICHAEL is alone in the now-deserted lobby, unwilling to go back. Then he goes to the door. He opens it a little. The sound of the trial. He opens the door fully. MICHAEL can see that it is ILANA who is testifying. The court is conspicuously packed. Large black-and-white photographs of the labor camp now dominate the room. MICHAEL comes quietly into the back of the room as the trial goes on.

MICHAEL has pushed past a couple of people to sit down near ROSE who is sitting in the body of the court. He looks across to the DEFENDANTS. RITA BECKHART, a large older woman, is one of a couple who isn't bothering to listen.

> PROSECUTOR
> In your book you describe the process of selection . . .

> ILANA
> Yes. You were made to work and then, when you were no longer any use to them, then they sent you back to Auschwitz to be killed.

> PROSECUTOR
> Are there people here today who made that selection?

> ILANA
> Yes.

> PROSECUTOR
> I need you to identify them. Can you please point them out?

ILANA points with her finger at the DEFENDANTS.

63

ILANA

Her. And her. And her. And her. And her. And her.

The last finger has been to HANNA. MICHAEL watches, but HANNA
does not react.

ILANA

Each of the guards would choose a certain num-
ber of women. Hanna Schmitz chose differently.

JUDGE

In what way differently?

ILANA

She had favorites. Girls, mostly young. We all re-
marked on it, she gave them food and places to
sleep. In the evening, she asked them to join her.
We all thought—well, you can imagine what we
thought.

HANNA stares back, impassive. MICHAEL watches.

ILANA

Then we found out—she was making these women
read aloud to her. They were reading to her. At first
we thought this guard, this guard is more sensitive,
she's more human, she's kinder. Often she chose the
weak, the sick—she picked them out, she seemed to
be protecting them almost. But then she dispatched
them. Is that kinder?

HANNA looks back, not apologizing.

INT. LOBBY. TOWN HALL. DAY

MICHAEL sits alone, head in hands, in despair.

64

INT. COURTROOM. DAY

Now ROSE is testifying. The court is quiet, focused.

> JUDGE
>
> I want to move on now to the march. As I under-
> stand it, you and your daughter were marched for
> many months.

> ROSE
>
> Yes. It was the winter of 1944. Our camp was
> closed down, we were told we had to move on.
> But the plan kept changing every day. Women
> were dying all around us in the snow. Half of us
> died on the march. My daughter says in the book,
> less a death march, more a death gallop.

MICHAEL looks along the row to where ILANA is now sitting.

> JUDGE
>
> Please tell us about the night in the church.

MICHAEL watches as ROSE looks across to ILANA. ILANA stares back
at her. MICHAEL watches the exchange as ROSE nods, as if accepting she
must go ahead and speak.

> ROSE
>
> That night we actually thought we were lucky be-
> cause we had a roof over our heads. We'd arrived
> in a village, as always, the guards took the best
> quarters, they took the priest's house. But they let
> us sleep in a church. There was a bombing raid.
> In the middle of the night. At first we could only
> hear the fire, it was in the steeple. Then we could
> see burning beams, and they began to crash to the
> floor. Everyone rushed, rushed to the doors. But
> the doors had been locked on the outside.

JUDGE

The church burned down? Nobody came to open
the doors? Is that right?

ROSE

Nobody.

JUDGE

Even though you were all burning to death?

ROSE nods.

JUDGE

How many people were killed?

ROSE

Everyone was killed.

JUDGE

How did you survive?

ROSE

I needed to get away from the other women. Because they were panicking, they were screaming.
I couldn't stand it. I couldn't stand their screaming. I was more frightened of the other women
than I was of the fire. So I took my daughter and
led her to the upper floor. I can't defend what I did.
It's impossible to defend. I took Ilana in my arms
and I led her towards the fire. There was a small
gallery at the side of the church on the upper level.
It saved our lives. The gallery didn't burn.

ROSE turns, in tears, to look at ILANA.

JUDGE

Thank you. I want to thank you for coming to this
country today to testify.

INT. LECTURE ROOM. LAW SCHOOL. DAY

The group is back in the big hall. But the atmosphere is grim. It's a while
before DIETER speaks.

DIETER

I don't know. I don't know what we're doing any
more.

ROHL

Don't you?

DIETER

You keep telling us to think like lawyers, but
there's something disgusting about this.

ROHL is very still, like an analyst who is finally leading his patient to the
heart of things.

ROHL

How so?

DIETER

This didn't happen to the Germans. It happened
to the Jews.

Everyone is shocked at his violent passion.

DIETER

What are we trying to do?

MICHAEL

We're trying to understand.

DIETER

Six women locked three hundred Jews in a church and let them burn. What is there to understand? Tell me, I'm asking: what is there to understand?

MICHAEL can't answer. DIETER gets up, outraged now.

DIETER

I started out believing in this trial, I thought it was great, now I think it's just a diversion.

ROHL

Yes? Diversion from what?

DIETER

You choose six women, you put them on trial, you say "They were the evil ones, they were the guilty ones." Brilliant! Because one of the victims happened to write a book! That's why they're on trial and nobody else. Do you know how many camps there were in Europe?

DIETER turns, furious.

DIETER

People go on about how much did everyone know? "Who knew?" "What did they know?" That isn't the question. The question is "How could you let it happen?" And better: 'Why didn't you kill yourself when you found out?'

One of the group walks out.

Thousands! That's how many. There were thousands of camps. Everyone knew.

DIETER'S passion is so great that everyone is shaken.

DIETER

Look at that woman . . .

MICHAEL

Which woman?

DIETER

The woman you're always staring at. I'm sorry,
but you are.

MICHAEL is white. The atmosphere is electric.

MICHAEL

I don't know which woman you mean.

DIETER

You know what I'd do? Put the gun in my hand,
I'd shoot her myself.

EXT. EMPTY ROAD. DAY

MICHAEL walks along an empty wooded road, miles from anywhere. The
sun is shining through the trees behind him.

EXT. STRUTHOF CAMP. DAY

The wire fence of a concentration camp, deserted. MICHAEL, with a back
pack, goes alone through the metal gate. MICHAEL walks among the deserted
empty huts.

INT. STRUTHOF CAMP. DAY

Inside one of the huts, MICHAEL is by himself staring at a line of empty beds. He moves on, overwhelmed, lost. He passes through the showers. Then he comes to a room with vast metal cages on either side. In the cages, the countless dusty shoes of the exterminated.

INT. STRUTHOF CAMP. DAY

MICHAEL opens a door and walks into a room with a line of gas ovens. He walks past them. Then he stands beside them, his head down.

INT. COURTROOM. DAY

HANNA is standing, being examined by the JUDGE. Large photographs and maps of the village, with the lay-out of the church, are now on display.

> JUDGE
> Why did you not unlock the doors?

He waits. HANNA doesn't reply.

> JUDGE
> Why did you not unlock the doors?

The JUDGE turns to the row of DEFENDANTS.

> JUDGE
> I've asked all of you and I'm getting no answer.
> Two of the victims are in this court. They deserve
> an answer.

ILANA and ROSE are not far away from MICHAEL and the STUDENTS. The JUDGE puts down a bound handwritten document.

                        JUDGE
        Here, this is the SS report. You all have copies.

There is a flurry of paperwork among the DEFENDANTS and LAWYERS
as they turn to their copies.

                        JUDGE
        This is the report which was written, approved
        and signed by all of you immediately after the
        event. In the written report, you all claim you
        didn't even know about the fire until after it hap-
        pened. But that isn't true, is it?

The JUDGE waits.

                        JUDGE
        Well? It isn't true.

                        HANNA
        I don't know what you're asking.

                        JUDGE
        The first thing I'm asking is, why didn't you un-
        lock the doors?

HANNA takes a look to the other DEFENDANTS. For the first time her
poise is crumbling.

                        HANNA
        Obviously. For the obvious reason. We couldn't.

                        JUDGE
        Why? Why couldn't you?

                        HANNA
        We were guards. Our job was to guard the prison-
        ers. We couldn't just let them escape.

JUDGE

I see. And if they escaped, then you'd be blamed,
you'd be charged, you might even be executed?

HANNA

No.

JUDGE

Well then?

The JUDGE waits.

HANNA

If we opened the doors, then there would have been
chaos. How could we have restored order? It happened so fast. It was snowing. The bombs . . . There
were flames all over the village. Then the screaming began. It got worse and worse. And if they'd
all come rushing out, we couldn't just let them escape. We couldn't. We were responsible for them.

JUDGE

So you did know what was happening? You did
know? You made a choice. You let them die
rather than risk letting them escape.

HANNA can't answer—she has no answer.

JUDGE

The other defendants have made an allegation
against you. Have you heard this allegation?

HANNA does not reply.

JUDGE

They say you were in charge.

HANNA

It isn't true. I was just one of the guards.

The other DEFENDANTS interrupt to call out, "She was in charge."

JUDGE

Did you write the report?

HANNA

No. No. We all discussed what to say. We all wrote
it together.

BECKHART

She wrote it! She wrote the report. She was in
charge.

JUDGE

Is that true?

HANNA

No. And I didn't write the report. Does it matter
who did?

RITA BECKHART has called out from her place. The JUDGE looks at
HANNA a moment.

JUDGE

I need to see a sample of your handwriting.

HANNA

My handwriting?

JUDGE

Yes. I need to establish who wrote the report.

At once HANNA'S COUNSEL rises.

HANNA'S COUNSEL

I'm sorry, but I really don't see how that's appropriate. Nearly twenty years have gone by.

JUDGE

Somebody take her this piece of paper.

HANNA'S COUNSEL

Are you really going to compare handwriting of
twenty years ago, with handwriting of today?

JUDGE

Give her the paper. Counsel, approach the bench.

A piece of paper and a pen are put down in front of HANNA. Her COUN-
SEL moves to the bench. MICHAEL stares, first at her, then at the pen and
paper, an apprehension rising in him.

INT & EXT. DAY AND NIGHT. FLASHBACKS

MICHAEL thinks back, to HANNA in her bedroom saying 'No you read',
to her looking puzzled at the menu on the bicycle trip, and to her throw-
ing a book away in the apartment. At this moment, MICHAEL realises she
is illiterate.

INT. COURTROOM. DAY

Back in the courtroom, HANNA looks up to the JUDGE to stop the
conference.

HANNA

There's no need. I wrote the report.

MICHAEL, in a panic, pushes along his row, past ROHL and the others, who all look up, knowing something is going on. HANNA turns, as if sensing him behind her.

INT. STAIRS. HEIDELBERG LAW SCHOOL. DAY

MICHAEL is sitting on the steps outside the lecture room. ROHL walks straight past him.

ROHL

You've been skipping seminars.

INT. LECTURE ROOM. HEIDELBERG LAW SCHOOL. DAY

MICHAEL comes into the room and sits down, smoking a cigarette. ROHL waits.

ROHL

So?

MICHAEL looks at him.

MICHAEL

I have a piece of information. Concerning one of
the defendants. Something they're not admitting.

ROHL

What information?

MICHAEL stubs out his cigarette.

ROHL

You don't need me to tell you. It's perfectly clear
you have a moral obligation to disclose it to the
court.

MICHAEL

It happens this information is favourable to the
defendant. It can help her case. It may even affect
the outcome, certainly the sentencing.

ROHL

So?

MICHAEL

There's a problem. The defendant herself is deter-
mined to keep this information secret.

Two STUDENTS come in for the seminar.

ROHL

A moment, please. Please.

Chastened, they leave.

ROHL

What are her reasons?

MICHAEL

Because she's ashamed.

ROHL

Ashamed? Ashamed of what?

MICHAEL doesn't answer.

ROHL

Have you spoken to her?

MICHAEL

Of course not.

ROHL

Why of course not?

MICHAEL

I can't. I can't do that. I can't talk to her.

ROHL

What we feel isn't important. It's utterly unim-
portant. The only question is what we do.

ROHL gets up.

ROHL

If people like you don't learn from what happened
to people like me, then what the hell is the point
of anything?

INT. REMAND CELL. EVENING

HANNA is sitting on the edge of her bed. A GUARD comes to the door.

GUARD

You have a visitor. Michael Berg.

HANNA is taken aback for a moment. Then she gets up.

EXT. PRISON WAITING ROOM. DAY

MICHAEL is standing smoking a cigarette in the waiting area. A whole num-
ber of visitors, old people, children, families are waiting. Some kids are playing with a football. Then a GUARD arrives and calls out names. MICHAEL's
name is called.

INT. MEETING ROOM. PRISON. DAY

HANNA is led swiftly down a prison corridor toward her meeting and sat down at a desk to wait.

EXT. PRISON YARD. DAY

MICHAEL is led in the GROUP towards the visiting room. It has come on to snow. As he walks towards the room, he loses heart. He changes his mind. The rest of the GROUP go on, as he falls behind, watching them go. He begins to turn back.

INT. MEETING ROOM. PRISON. DAY.

HANNA sits down at the empty table, waiting.

EXT. PRISON YARD. DAY

MICHAEL turns away and heads back the way he came.

INT. MEETING ROOM. PRISON. DAY

HANNA looks round. Nobody is coming. She waits more.

                    GUARD
          Time's up.

INT. PRISON. EVENING

HANNA is still waiting. Then she is led back to her cell.

INT. MARTHE'S ROOM. STUDENT DIGS. NIGHT

MICHAEL appears at the door of MARTHE'S room. She is working at her desk. He smiles and closes the door.

MARTHE
You've taken your time.

They kiss. She starts to pull his clothes off. He lets her. He makes no move to undress her. She takes all his clothes off until he is naked, and she remains clothed. He looks at her a moment, then takes her in his arms and they go down on the bed. They make love.

INT. MARTHE'S ROOM. NIGHT

MARTHE is apparently asleep, MICHAEL awake. As quietly as he can MICHAEL tries to slip away.

MARTHE
Where are you going?

MICHAEL
I'm sorry. I need to sleep by myself.

INT. REMAND CELL. DAWN

HANNA is standing naked at the sink, preparing herself for the day.

INT. STUDENT DIGS. MICHAEL'S ROOM. DAWN

MICHAEL is lying in his own bed, staring up at the ceiling, not able to sleep. MICHAEL reluctantly pushes back the cover and gets naked out of bed. Slowly he begins to dress.

INT. REMAND CELL. DAY

HANNA washes herself, naked.

INT. STUDENT DIGS. DAY

MICHAEL is dressed now. He stands in front of his mirror, adjusting his tie.

INT. REMAND CELL. DAY

HANNA stands in front of the mirror, tying her tie. There is a small, in-adequate mirror in which she checks her dress—a black suit, a white blouse and black tie. She looks very formal.

INT. PRISON. DAY

HANNA is led through the prison by a GUARD.

EXT. TOWN HALL. DAY

A lot of people heading into the courtroom. As the seminar group goes in, MICHAEL hangs back. ROHL looks at him as he goes through the doors. MICHAEL is left outside, then goes to watch as the vans arrive.

INT. COURTROOM. TOWN HALL. DAY

HANNA and the PRISONERS are led into the court. HANNA'S suit is so formal that members of the public call out. 'Nazi! Nazi!' DIETER leans in to MARTHE. HANNA walks on to her place.

INT. COURTROOM. DAY

Everyone rises as the JUDGES come in to take their places. HANNA's face is resigned, without expression. The JUDGES sit. The whole court goes quiet.

JUDGE

The court finds guilty the defendants Rita Beckhart, Karolina Steinhof, Regina Kreutz, Angela
Zieber, Andrea Luhmann jointly aiding and abet-
ting murder in three hundred cases. The court
finds the defendant Hanna Schmitz guilty of murder in three hundred cases.

There are tears in MICHAEL's eyes as he watches.

JUDGE

The court sentences the accused as follows. Rita
Beckhart, Karolina Steinhof, Regina Kreutz, Angela Zieber, and Andrea Luhmann, you will each
serve a total sentence in prison of four years and
three months.

ROHL, MARTHE, DIETER and the students are looking down on the sentencing. MICHAEL is crying.

JUDGE

Hanna Schmitz, in view of your own admissions
and your special role, you are in a different cate-
gory. The court sentences the accused Schmitz to
imprisonment for life.

HANNA is impassive, not reacting. Then she turns and looks up to the gallery.

EXT. COURTHOUSE. DAY

MICHAEL walks away through the cameras and news crews.

INT. TRAIN. DAY

MICHAEL sits on the train, thinking. The younger MICHAEL becomes
the old.

INT. TRAIN. DAY

1976. MICHAEL is sitting beside JULIA. MICHAEL is 32, JULIA is a bright little 4-year-old in a coat. The countryside speeding by.

> JULIA
> Where are we going?

> MICHAEL
> I said: I'll tell you when we get there. You told me
> you liked surprises.

> JULIA
> I like surprises.

EXT. BLUMENSTRASSE. DAY

MICHAEL walks with JULIA towards their old house. He looks round, the memory of coming with HANNA as a sick boy 18 years earlier clear in his mind. The same landmarks.

INT. DINING ROOM. BERG APARTMENT. DAY

They are all three eating at the dinner table, eating a small roast chicken.

> MICHAEL
> She's grown, hasn't she?

> CARLA
> I don't know. It's so long since I saw her, Michael,
> how can I tell?

> MICHAEL
> My fault. We shouldn't have come unannounced.

JULIA

Daddy, why's she angry?

MICHAEL smiles. Even CARLA smiles slightly.

MICHAEL

I'm afraid I've have some bad news. Julia knows.
We've already told her. Gertrud and I are getting
a divorce.

JULIA

Daddy's going to live in his own house.

CARLA

You didn't come for your father's funeral, but you
come for this?

MICHAEL

You know, it's not easy for me to visit this town.

CARLA

Were you really so unhappy?

MICHAEL

That's not what I'm saying. It's not what I meant.

CARLA

Well then?

CARLA looks at him hard.

MICHAEL

You mustn't worry about Gertrud. I'm going to
look after her. And anyway, let's face it, she's already a state prosecutor, she earns far more than
I do.

CARLA

Michael, I'm not worried about Gertrud. I'm
worried about you.

INT. TRAIN. EVENING

Exhausted by her day, JULIA is sleeping in MICHAEL'S arms. He looks
down at her, full of love.

EXT. SCHONEBERG. BERLIN. NIGHT

On the other side of a busy Berlin street full of traffic, MICHAEL holds
JULIA'S hand, a loving father, to guide her across the street.

INT. LANDING. GERTRUD'S APARTMENT. BERLIN. NIGHT

GERTRUD has come to the door, a shrewd-looking intelligent woman, a
little older than MICHAEL, very thin, in slacks and a blouse. MICHAEL
is standing outside with JULIA.

JULIA

Hello, Mummy.

GERTRUD

Hello, beautiful.

GERTRUD leans down and scoops JULIA up, kisses her. MICHAEL stands
on the step, hovering.

GERTRUD

Do you mind if I don't ask you in?

MICHAEL

I don't mind at all. I've a lot to do, in fact.

It doesn't look like it. He stands, not going.

MICHAEL

I took her to see where I grew up.

GERTRUD

You went to the West? My God, what a trip.

JULIA

We went to say hello to Granny.

GERTRUD

Oh. Daddy took you to see Carla, did he?

JULIA

She was strange.

GERTRUD

Come on, let's see what's on TV.

GERTRUD gives JULIA her supper and puts her in front of the TV. Then she comes back to MICHAEL.

GERTRUD

I bet she was strange.

MICHAEL

You could say.

GERTRUD

She always was. Why on earth did you decide to do that?

MICHAEL

I don't know. Impulse.

GERTRUD says nothing.

MICHAEL

I suppose if I'm honest, we went because I wanted
to re-establish contact.

GERTRUD

With your mother? And did you succeed?

They both smile.

MICHAEL

Are you all right?

He touches her arm.

GERTRUD

Michael, you're meant to be an intelligent man.
Don't you know, it's very hard to receive contact
if you're not willing to give it?

GERTRUD looks level, not unkind.

GERTRUD

Say good-bye to Julia.

JULIA

Good-bye, Daddy.

MICHAEL turns to say good-bye.

INT. MICHAEL'S APARTMENT. KREUZBERG. NIGHT

MICHAEL standing in the empty room. It's eerily silent. He goes to his
bookcase. He runs his fingers along the spines, as HANNA once did. He
takes out a paperback of *The Odyssey*. He looks at it a moment, then he starts
to read to himself.

"Sing to me of the Man, Muse, the man of twists
and turns
Driven time and again off course, once he had
plundered
The hallowed heights of Troy . . ."

He sits back.

INT. HANNA'S CELL. DAWN

HANNA is in her cell, folding her blanket. She is 53, a new austerity, a greyness about her. Her cell is modern, but without decoration.

INT. PRISON. CORRIDOR. DAY

A GUARD comes along the corridor, calling out "Mail." She leans into Hanna's cell to tell her she has mail. HANNA is obviously surprised.

INT. MAIL ROOM. PRISON. DAY

HANNA reports to the mail room where she is given a big parcel, which she is told to open. Inside, a huge batch of casette tapes and a tape machine.

INT. CELL. DAY

HANNA is opening the box, taking out the tapes.

INT. MICHAEL'S APARTMENT. EVENING

MICHAEL gets out a tape machine.

INT. CELL. DAY

In her cell HANNA takes out the machine.

INT. MICHAEL'S APARTMENT. EVENING

MICHAEL holds the microphone.

MICHAEL

Testing. Testing. 1—2—3.

INT. CELL. DAY

HANNA puts a cassette into the machine.

MICHAEL'S VOICE

The Odyssey by Homer.

In panic, she turns it off.

INT. MICHAEL'S APARTMENT. EVENING

MICHAEL presses the recording button and speaks into the machine.

MICHAEL

The Odyssey by Homer.
"Sing to me of the Man, Muse, the man of twists
and turns
Driven time and again off course, once he had
plundered
The hallowed heights of Troy . . .

Many cities of men he saw and learned their
minds,
Many pains he suffered, heartsick at the open sea,
Fighting to save his life and bring his comrades
home . . ."

INT. MICHAEL'S APARTMENT. NIGHT

Later. MICHAEL is now walking up and down, in his shorts and T-shirt,
microphone in hand, still reading.

> MICHAEL
>
> "Ah, how shameless—the way these mortals blame
> the gods.
> From us alone, they say, come all their miseries . . ."

INT. BEDROOM. NIGHT

Middle of the night. MICHAEL is lying on his back, still reading.

> MICHAEL
>
> "Who are you? Where are you from? Your city?
> Your parents?
> I'm wonderstruck—you drank my drugs, you're
> not bewitched . . ."

INT. LIVING ROOM. DAY

MICHAEL takes a cassette and puts it into a white box. He writes on the
side ODYSSEY 6. Then he reaches up to put it on a shelf next to boxes sep-
arately marked ODYSSEY 1,2,3,4,5. Then he takes out a small notebook
and cross-references the new tape in a handwritten list.

INT. CELL. NIGHT

It's dark. HANNA is lying on the bed.

> MICHAEL'S VOICE
> "Zeus from the very start, the thunder king
> Has hated the race of Atreus with a vengeance—
> His trustiest weapon women's twisted wiles . . ."

HANNA smiles with pleasure at his reading.

INT & EXT. MONTAGE. DAY & NIGHT

A montage of MICHAEL reading and HANNA listening. MICHAEL is reading different books. He is animated now, excited. There are extracts from *The Old Man and the Sea* (Hemingway), *Anatol* (Schnitzler), *The World of Yesterday* (Zweig) and *Doctor Zhivago* (Pasternak). MICHAEL catching fire with excitement with what he is doing. HANNA collecting the tapes from the mail room and organizing on her shelves—her library growing.

INT. CELL. NIGHT

HANNA is lying in bed listening to a new tape.

> MICHAEL
> *The Lady with the Little Dog,* by Anton Chekhov.
> "The talk was that a new face had appeared on the promenade, a lady with a little dog . . ."

EXT. EXERCISE YARD. PRISON. DAY

HANNA is walking round with other PRISONERS, in sequence. Suddenly she stops dead, an idea hitting her.

INT. PRISON LIBRARY. DAY

The library is right next to the mail room. HANNA walks past the mail room and goes to the library counter.

> HANNA
> I want to take out a book.

> LIBRARIAN
> Which book?

> HANNA
> Do you have *The Lady with the Little Dog?*

> LIBRARIAN
> What's your name?

> HANNA
> Hanna Schmitz.

The LIBRARIAN goes to get it. HANNA stands, waiting, and looks at the stacks of books, for the first time seeing possibility.

INT. CELL. DAY

HANNA is back in the cell. She puts down a new parcel and a book. She puts the parcel to one side, then opens the book. She then winds back the tape which is already in the recorder.

> MICHAEL'S VOICE
> *The Lady with the Little Dog*, a story by Anton Chekhov. "The talk was . . ."

She turns off the tape. She runs her finger along the title "The Lady with the Little Dog." She gets down a small decorated metal tin, and takes a pencil from it. She starts making the sounds. "The," "the," "the" . . . L, L, L, etc.

INT. CELL. NIGHT

HANNA is working now, circling the word "the" each time it comes in the book. The book is covered in marks.

EXT & INT. MICHAEL'S APARTMENT. EVENING

1981. MICHAEL is coming down a busy Kreuzberg street. He is 37. He goes into his block. He opens the door: the place is much more lived-in. He picks up his mail. Thumbing through it, he sees a letter in childish handwriting. MICHAEL frowns, opening it and taking out a piece of paper.

INT. MICHAEL'S APARTMENT. EVENING

MICHAEL is holding a letter. He looks down at the writing: "Thanks for the latest, kid. I really liked it." He stares, then puts it down and steps back stunned.

INT. CELL. DAY

HANNA stands with a new package. She opens it excitedly. She takes out tapes. She looks for writing, a letter. There is none. She turns the packing paper over and over, but there's nothing. She stands, desolate.

INT. CELL. PRISON. NIGHT. MONTAGE

HANNA effortfully writing various letters—just a single message on each. The pen working agonizingly across the paper. First:

I WOULD LIKE MORE ROMANCE, LESS ADVENTURE

Next:

I AM NOT SURE WHAT KAFKA IS SAYING

INT. MICHAEL'S APARTMENT. BEDROOM. NIGHT

MICHAEL continuing to read to her on the machine.

INT. CELL. PRISON. NIGHT. MONTAGE

HANNA still writing.

DO YOU STILL LIKE DICKENS?

Then finally, many attempts at the same sentence, written many times:

DO YOU RECEIVE MY LETTERS? WRITE TO ME, KID

INT. STUDY. MICHAEL'S APARTMENT. DAY

MICHAEL is reading the latest letter from HANNA. He looks at it. "Do you receive my letters? Write to me, kid." MICHAEL opens a drawer in a file box on the floor. There is a stack of her letters inside. He puts the latest on top of the pile and closes the drawer.

INT. CELL. PRISON. DAY

HANNA stands at her window, in despair.

INT. MICHAEL'S APARTMENT. KREUZBERG. DAY

1988. MICHAEL, 44, is at his desk, with the phone in his hand, with a typed letter in front of him.

MS. BRENNER (VOICE ON PHONE)

You're Michael Berg?

MICHAEL'S VOICE

Yes.

MS. BRENNER (VOICE ON PHONE)

You got my letter?

MICHAEL

I have it here.

MS. BRENNER (PHONE)

As I say, Hanna Schmitz is coming up for release
very soon.

MICHAEL fingers the letter a moment.

INT. BRENNER'S OFFICE. PRISON. DAY

MS. BRENNER is sitting at her desk in a simple, modern office.

MS. BRENNER

Hanna has been in prison for over twenty years.
She has no family. She has no friends. You're her
only contact. And I'm told you don't visit her.

INT. MICHAEL'S APARTMENT. KREUZBERG. DAY

MICHAEL is sitting quite still.

MICHAEL

No. I don't.

INT. BRENNER'S OFFICE. DAY

> MS. BRENNER
> When she gets out, she's going to need a job.
> She's going to need somewhere to live. You can't
> imagine how frightening the modern world will
> seem to her.

There is a silence.

> MICHAEL
> Yes. I'm still here.

INT. MICHAEL'S APARTMENT. KREUZBERG. DAY

> MS. BRENNER
> I have no one else to ask. If you don't take respon-
> sibility for her, then Hanna has no future at all.

> MICHAEL
> It's kind of you. Thank you for letting me know.

MICHAEL puts the phone down. He looks as if he has just been handed a
sentence. He gets up and stares at the wall which is now stacked with all
the books he has read. Then he goes to his balcony.

EXT & INT. MICHAEL'S APARTMENT. KREUZBERG. DAY

MICHAEL stands looking out over Berlin from his balcony.

EXT. PRISON. DAY

MICHAEL walks along the road by the prison wall, then goes to the guichet
to sign in.

EXT. PRISON YARD. DAY

MICHAEL is waiting in a small barred waiting area as MS. BRENNER walks across the yard to open the gate and let MICHAEL in.

> MS. BRENNER
> You're Michael Berg?

> MICHAEL
> Yes.

> MS. BRENNER
> Louisa Brenner. We were expecting you earlier.

INT & EXT. STAIRS & PASSAGE. PRISON. DAY

MS. BRENNER is walking MICHAEL up the steps towards the prison canteen. They pass GUARDS and INMATES.

> MS. BRENNER
> I should warn you: for a long time Hanna held
> herself together. She was very purposeful. In the
> last few years she's different. She's let herself go.

INT. CANTEEN. PRISON. DAY

MS. BRENNER leads MICHAEL to the door of the canteen.

> MS. BRENNER
> They're in the canteen. They're just finishing
> lunch.

MICHAEL sees an OLD WOMAN who is sitting at a table. Her blue dress is stretched too tight across her heavy body. Her hair is grey. She has a book

in her lap, but she's not reading it. A few PRISONERS are finishing their
meal.

It takes MICHAEL a moment to realise the OLD WOMAN is HANNA.
Then HANNA becomes aware of being watched. She turns and looks round.
At once her face lights up. MICHAEL smiles back, but as he approaches her,
he fixes onto her inquiring look and sees the light go out of her eyes, as if
she has looked at him and been disappointed. He sits down opposite her.
She smiles, weary.

> HANNA
>
> You've grown up, kid.

She takes his hand. There is a long silence, MICHAEL unable to think of
anything to say. He withdraws his hand.

> MICHAEL
>
> I've got a friend who's a tailor, he makes my suits.
> He'll give you a job. And I've found you some-
> where to live. It's a nice place. Quite small but
> nice. I think you'll like it.

> HANNA
>
> Thank you.

There's a moment's silence.

> MICHAEL
>
> There are various social programs, cultural stuff I
> can sign you up for. And there's a public library
> very close.

HANNA nods slightly.

> MICHAEL
>
> You read a lot?

HANNA

I prefer being read to.

There is a short silence.

HANNA

That's over now, isn't it?

MICHAEL doesn't answer.

HANNA

Did you get married?

MICHAEL

I did. Yes I did. We have a daughter. I'm not seeing as much of her as I would like. I'd like to see a
great deal more of her.

After a few moments, he concedes.

MICHAEL

The marriage didn't last.

There is a silence.

MICHAEL

Have you spent a lot of time thinking about the
past?

HANNA

You mean, with you?

MICHAEL

No. No, I didn't mean with me.

HANNA

Before the trial I never thought about the past. I
never had to.

MICHAEL

And now? What do you feel now?

HANNA looks a moment, a haunting look, searching him.

HANNA

It doesn't matter what I think. It doesn't matter
what I feel. The dead are still dead.

There's a silence.

MICHAEL

I wasn't sure what you'd learned.

HANNA

I have learned, kid. I've learned to read.

MICHAEL stares, devastated.

MICHAEL

I'll pick you up next week, OK?

HANNA

That sounds a good plan.

MICHAEL

Good. Quietly, or shall we make a big fuss?

HANNA

Quietly.

MICHAEL

OK. Quietly.

They look at each other. The other PRISONERS have already gone. They
stand up. She scans his face again, searching for his thoughts. He takes her
in his arms, a little awkward.

Take care, kid.

MICHAEL

You too.

They walk side by side, back towards the door. Then by way of saying good-bye, she takes his hand.

MICHAEL

See you next week.

She stretches her arm out before she lets go of his hand, then vanishes inside. MICHAEL walks on alone.

EXT. PRISON. EVENING

MICHAEL comes out of the main entrance. He stands a moment, looking round at the evening. MICHAEL walks to his car.

INT. HANNA'S ROOM. EVENING

The room is simple, a bedroom to one side, a bathroom to the other. It is all furnished with simple functional furniture. The end of a hard day's work. MICHAEL hangs a picture over the desk—a landscape, reminiscent of where they once went cycling. The job is done. He looks round, grimly content.

INT. CELL. DAWN

HANNA is lying on her bed, fully dressed. She gets up and gets some books down from the shelf. She puts them, one by one, in a pile on the table. Then she takes off her shoes. She stands up and climbs onto the pile of books on the table. Her bare feet on the books. Then she reaches up.

EXT & INT. PRISON. DAY

MICHAEL gets out of the car. He is carrying a bunch of flowers. He walks towards the prison. He leans in to the GUARD who is in a modern office.

INT. PRISON. DAY

From the far end of the corridor, MICHAEL is seen sitting on a bench. MS. BRENNER comes out of her office and murmurs in his ear. MICHAEL is seen nodding, ashen.

INT. CORRIDOR & CELL. PRISON. DAY

The two of them come together down the corridor. They stop at the open door of the cell. The body has been removed. The books are still on the floor. MICHAEL goes in. A bare table, a chair, a bed, a closet, a toilet in the corner behind the door. There are shelves with books, an alarm clock, a stuffed bear, two mugs, instant coffee, tea-tins.

MICHAEL
She didn't pack. She never intended to leave.

MS. BRENNER looks at him in confirmation. MICHAEL looks at the two lower shelves on which are arranged the tapes with the cassette machine.

Above the bed are a series of cuttings, pictures torn from magazines, showing meadows, hillsides, pasture, cherry trees. One in particular: a burst of autumnal colours. MICHAEL kneels on the bed to look at them. There are quotations, articles, recipes, even sayings in HANNA'S childish handwriting: "Spring lets its blue banner flutter through the air" is one. Then he sees a newspaper photograph: the young MICHAEL BERG receiving a prize from the school principal. The headline MICHAEL BERG RECEIVES SCHOOL LITERATURE PRIZE.

MS. BRENNER reaches out for a tea-tin from the shelf. Then she sits next to MICHAEL on the bed, and takes out a folded sheet of paper from her suit pocket.

>   MS. BRENNER
> She left me a message, a sort of will. I'll read out
> the bit that concerns you.

MICHAEL looks at the effortful handwriting on the page.

>   MS. BRENNER
> "There is money in the old tea-tin. Give it to
> Michael Berg. He should send it, alongside the
> 7,000 marks in the bank, to the daughter who
> wrote the book. It's for her. She should decide
> what to do with it. And tell Michael I said hello.
> Tell him to get on with his life."

MS. BRENNER looks at him.

>   MS. BRENNER
> Do you want to see her?

MICHAEL shakes his head.

EXT. BRIDGE. MANHATTAN. DAY

MICHAEL rides in a taxi into Manhattan. A view of the familiar skyline.

EXT. FIFTH AVENUE. DAY

MICHAEL'S taxi comes up Fifth Avenue. It draws up outside an expensive apartment block. MICHAEL gets out and goes in, the Manhattan skyline opening up behind him.

INT. LIVING ROOM. ILANA'S APARTMENT. DAY

A superbly appointed space full of great and expensive art. MICHAEL has taken his coat off. ILANA MATHER appears, elegant, well-dressed—on the surface, the spirit of prosperous New York. She is now in her early fifties.

MICHAEL

Ms. Mather?

ILANA

Yes. You're Michael Berg. I was expecting you.

ILANA

So you must tell me: what exactly brings you to the United States?

MICHAEL

I was already here. I was at a conference in Boston.

ILANA

You're a lawyer?

MICHAEL

Yes.

ILANA

I was intrigued by your letter, but I can't say I wholly understood it. You attended the trial?

MICHAEL

Yes. Almost twenty years ago. I was a law student. I remember you, I remember your mother very clearly.

ILANA

My mother died in Israel—a good many years ago.

103

MICHAEL

I'm sorry.

MICHAEL hesitates for a moment.

ILANA

Go on, please.

MICHAEL

Perhaps you heard. Hanna Schmitz recently died.
She killed herself.

ILANA shakes her head.

ILANA

She was a friend of yours?

MICHAEL

A kind of friend. It's as simple as this. Hanna was
illiterate for the greater part of her life.

ILANA

Is that an explanation of her behaviour?

MICHAEL

No.

ILANA

Or an excuse?

MICHAEL shakes his head.

MICHAEL

No. No. She taught herself to read when she was
in prison. I sent her tapes. She'd always liked being read to.

ILANA shifts slightly.

>ILANA

Why don't you start by being honest with me? At least start that way. What was the nature of your friendship?

>MICHAEL

When I was young I had an affair with Hanna.

ILANA looks at him for a moment.

>ILANA

I'm not sure I can help you, Mr. Berg. Or rather, even if I could I'm not willing to.

>MICHAEL

I was almost sixteen when I took up with her. The affair only lasted a summer. But.

>ILANA

But what?

MICHAEL just looks at her.

>ILANA

I see. And did Hanna Schmitz acknowledge the effect she'd had on your life?

MICHAEL stares back, understood for the first time.

>MICHAEL

She'd done much worse to other people. I've never told anyone.

ILANA

People ask all the time what I learned in the
camps. But the camps weren't therapy. What do
you think these places were? Universities? We
didn't go there to learn. One becomes very clear
about these things.

ILANA looks at him, unrelenting.

ILANA

What are you asking for? Forgiveness for her? Or
do you just want to feel better yourself? My advice,
go to the theatre, if you want catharsis. Please. Go
to literature. Don't go to the camps. Nothing
comes out of the camps. Nothing.

ILANA looks at him, unrelenting.

MICHAEL

What she wanted . . . what she wanted was to
leave you her money. I have with me.

ILANA

To do what?

MICHAEL

As you think fit.

MICHAEL reaches for his briefcase. He takes out the lavender tea-tin, which
he sets down on the table in front of ILANA.

MICHAEL

Here.

ILANA lifts the tin.

ILANA

When I was a little girl, I had a tea-tin for my treasures. Not quite like this. It had Cyrillic lettering. I took it with me to the camp, but it got stolen.

MICHAEL

What was in it?

ILANA

Oh. Sentimental things. A piece of hair from our dog. Some tickets to operas my father had taken me to. It wasn't stolen for its contents. It was the tin itself which was valuable, what you could do with it.

She sits a moment, overcome, her hand on the tin.

ILANA

There's nothing I can do with this money. If I give it to anything associated with the extermination of the Jews, then to me it will seem like absolution and that is something I'm neither willing nor in a position to grant.

MICHAEL nods slightly.

MICHAEL

I was thinking maybe an organization to encourage literacy.

ILANA

Good.

There's a silence.

ILANA

Good.

MICHAEL

Do you know if there's a Jewish organization?

ILANA

I'll be surprised if there isn't. There's a Jewish or-
ganisation for everything. Not that illiteracy is a
very Jewish problem.

There is the shadow of a smile.

ILANA

Why don't you find out? Send them the money.

MICHAEL

Shall I do it in Hanna's name?

ILANA

As you think fit.

ILANA smiles slightly. She puts her hand on top of the tin.

ILANA

I'll keep the tin.

INT. ILANA'S HOUSE. DAY

ILANA is standing at the window watching down to the street where
MICHAEL is walking away. She has the tin in her hand. When he's van-
ished, she turns and goes into her bedroom. There on the dressing table, is
a framed photo of ILANA with her mother in Germany before the war. She
sets the tin down beside the photo.

INT & EXT. CAR. DAY

1995. MICHAEL is driving JULIA in the big Mercedes through the German countryside. He is tense, silent. JULIA takes a sideways look at him, but he does not respond.

> JULIA
>
> Where are we going?

> MICHAEL
>
> I thought you liked surprises.

> JULIA
>
> I do. I do like surprises.

EXT. COUNTRY. DAY

They draw up at a church. It is the same one he and HANNA passed on their bicycles years before. MICHAEL and JULIA get out and walk towards the graveyard at the side.

EXT. CEMETERY. DAY

MICHAEL & JULIA stand at a deserted grave-side. The whole cemetery is seen. MICHAEL stoops down and uncovers a simple stone: HANNA SCHMITZ 1923–1988. JULIA, watching, says her name.

> JULIA
>
> Hanna Schmitz.

JULIA waits a moment.

> JULIA
>
> Who was she?

MICHAEL

That's what I wanted to tell you. That's why we're
here.

JULIA looks, waiting. MICHAEL looks for a moment as if he will not go on.

JULIA

So tell me.

There is a moment, then they turn to stroll, MICHAEL talking, starting to
tell the story.

MICHAEL

I was 15, I was coming home from school, I was
ill . . .

They walk away among the trees.

FADE TO BLACK